EDGE BOOKS™

DINOSAUR WARS

TRICERATOPS

★★★★★★★★★★★

VS.

STEGOSAURUS

★★★★★★★★★★★

WHEN HORNS AND PLATES COLLIDE

by Michael O'Hearn

Consultant:
Mathew J. Wedel, PhD
Paleontologist and Assistant Professor
Western University of Health Sciences
Pomona, California

CAPSTONE PRESS
a capstone imprint

Edge Books are published by Capstone Press,
151 Good Counsel Drive, P.O. Box 669, Mankato, Minnesota 56002.
www.capstonepress.com

092009
005619WZS10

 Books published by Capstone Press are manufactured with paper
containing at least 10 percent post-consumer waste.

Library of Congress Cataloging-in-Publication Data
O'Hearn, Michael, 1972–
    Triceratops vs. Stegosaurus : when horns and plates collide / by
Michael O'Hearn.
    p. cm. — (Edge books. Dinosaur wars)
    Summary: "Describes the features of Triceratops and Stegosaurus,
and how they may have battled each other in prehistoric times" — Provided
by publisher.
    Includes bibliographical references and index.
    ISBN 978-1-4296-3938-5 (lib. bdg.)
    1. Triceratops — Juvenile literature. 2. Stegosaurus — Juvenile
literature. I. Title.
QE862.O65O34 2010
567.915'8 — dc22   2009028149

Editorial Credits
Aaron Sautter, editor; Kyle Grenz, designer; Marcie Spence, media researcher;
    Nathan Gassman, art director; Laura Manthe, production specialist

Illustrations
Philip Renne and Jon Hughes

Photo Credits
Shutterstock/Leigh Prather, stylized backgrounds
Shutterstock/Steve Cukrov, 18 (top)
Shutterstock/Valery Potapova, parchment backgrounds

TABLE OF CONTENTS

WELCOME TO DINOSAUR WARS!

Dinosaurs were brutal creatures. They fought each other and ate each other. Usually it was meat-eater versus plant-eater or big versus small. But in Dinosaur Wars, it's a free for all. Plant-eaters attack plant-eaters. Giants fight giants. And small dinosaurs gang up on huge opponents. In Dinosaur Wars, any dinosaur battle is possible!

In this dinosaur war, Triceratops and Stegosaurus collide. You'll see how these two plant-eaters could be downright brutal. You'll learn about their defensive abilities. You'll discover their wicked weapons. And while these two dinosaurs usually didn't try to pick fights, you'll find out how they may have brawled. Then you'll see them battling head-to-head — and you'll get to watch from a front row seat!

Triceratops (trye-SER-uh-tops)
Stegosaurus (STEG-uh-sore-uhs)

THE COMBATANTS

TRICERATOPS VS. STEGOSAURUS

Triceratops and Stegosaurus never actually butted heads. Stegosaurus died out about 144 million years ago. That was millions of years before the first Triceratops walked the earth. Triceratops lived from 70 million years ago until dinosaurs became **extinct** about 65 million years ago.

If Triceratops and Stegosaurus had lived at the same time, they probably would have bumped into each other. Both lived in the western United States. In fact, fossils of both dinosaurs were first discovered in Colorado.

But even if Triceratops and Stegosaurus had met, it's unlikely they would have battled. Both were **herbivores**. Their deadly weapons were used for defense rather than attacking.

Both Triceratops and Stegosaurus were named by scientist Othniel Charles Marsh. Marsh discovered more than 80 species of dinosaurs.

FIERCE FACT DISCOVERY

extinct — no longer living anywhere in the world

herbivore — an animal that eats only plants

SIZE

Triceratops
30 feet long; 10 tons

★ ★ ★ ★

★ ★ ★
Stegosaurus
30 feet long; 3 tons

At 30 feet (9 meters) long and weighing up to 10 tons (9 metric tons), Triceratops could bash through whatever got in his way. With his shield-like neck **frill**, Triceratops was built like a bulldozer. Triceratops' size and weight would be a big advantage in a fight.

frill — a bony collar that fans around an animal's neck

Stegosaurus was about as big as a school bus. He was 30 feet (9 meters) long and weighed about 3 tons (2.7 metric tons). But in the dinosaur world, Stegosaurus was far from being a giant. He was big enough to put up a good fight, but he would have trouble beating a larger opponent.

SPEED AND AGILITY

Stegosaurus was a clumsy runner. His back legs were twice as long as his front legs. This was not the best design for speed. But it pushed Stegosaurus' weight toward his backside so he could **pivot** quickly on his back legs. This movement helped him keep his mighty spiked tail between him and his enemies.

pivot — to turn on a central point

Triceratops was built like a rhino. His sturdy legs and broad feet supported his heavy, muscular body. Triceratops ran fast for his size, possibly up to 20 miles (32 kilometers) per hour. But he could not turn easily. He mainly just charged straight ahead. He was made to run into his enemies, not away from them.

WEAPONS

Stegosaurus had only one weapon, but it was deadly. His tail was powerful and dangerous. It had four hard, sharp spikes attached to the end. Each swordlike spike was up to 3 feet (1 meter) long. A swift strike from Stegosaurus' spiked tail could bring death to any opponent.

The name Triceratops means "three–horned face."

Triceratops had spikes of his own. Two horns stuck out above his eyes, and a third was at the tip of his snout. The snout horn was short, but it could cause great damage when crashing into an enemy. The upper horns were long and sharp. They could be driven into an enemy's body. Triceratops also had a sharp, powerful beak. It could deliver a painful bite. Of all the plant-eating dinosaurs, Triceratops was among the most dangerous.

DEFENSES

Triceratops Bony neck frill			
★	★	★	★

Stegosaurus Bony back plates				
★	★	★	★	★

Triceratops' bony neck frill extended from the top of his head. It acted like a shield to protect the dinosaur's neck. The frill was useful when Triceratops barreled into an opponent headfirst. Many fossils of Triceratops frills show battle scars. They prove that the neck frill was a valuable defense. The frill also may have made Triceratops look more dangerous to his enemies.

Stegosaurus had two rows of bony plates running along his back from his neck to his tail. Scientists once thought these plates laid flat on the dinosaur's back like armor. Today, scientists think the back plates stood upright for protection during attacks. The plates also may have helped different **species** tell one another apart.

species — a group of animals that share common characteristics

15

ATTACK STYLE

In a fight, Stegosaurus tried to keep enemies behind him. He moved sideways and in circles to line up opponents for his dangerous tail swing. Stegosaurus' tail was more flexible than the tails of most dinosaurs. He could whip it up and down and side to side to smash his opponents.

Dinosaur horns, spikes, and beaks were covered in a strong substance called keratin. Human fingernails are also made of keratin.

Triceratops kept his enemies in front of him where he could bash and bite them. All of his weapons were attached to his head. He needed to get up close to cause damage. He would charge with his head down to pierce an enemy with his horns. Afterward, he could bite his opponent with his powerful beak or keep stabbing with his horns.

17

GET READY TO RUMBLE!

Get ready for the rumble, the boom, and the crash! It's time for the thunder and the pain. These two dinosaurs don't just fight, they bash! In one corner is the mighty bulldozer — Triceratops! He's horned and heavy and ready to charge. In the other corner is the spiky challenger — Stegosaurus! He's a brawler with a deadly tail, and he's not afraid to use it. The winner of this knockout battle is anybody's guess.

TRICERATOPS

SIZE	SPEED AND AGILITY	WEAPONS	DEFENSES	ATTACK STYLE
★★★★ ★★★	★★★	★★★ ★★★	★★★ ★★★★★	★★★ ★★★

STEGOSAURUS

You've got a front row seat. So grab your favorite snack and drink, turn the page, and get ready to enjoy the battle!

ONE LAST THING...

This battle is made up. It's fake. These dinos never fought. And even if they did, no one knows how it would have happened. Nobody knows which dinosaur would have won. But if you like a good battle, this one should be a smash!

PAIN

It's early in the morning. The sky is gray. Swirls of mist hang in the air. Stegosaurus stands at the edge of a clearing, munching on some leaves. He hears something rustling in the bushes nearby. He slowly cranes his neck to look in the direction of the sound. He keeps chewing leaves while staring at some ferns across the clearing.

Ferns are his favorite meal, so Stegosaurus slowly walks toward them. When he gets close, he sees the plants sway back and forth. He hears heavy breathing and a snapping sound.

Stegosaurus ignores the sounds and reaches down for a mouthful of ferns. He takes one bite and then another. Suddenly a giant, horned head pops up from the leafy plants. It's Triceratops, and he isn't happy.

FIERCE FACT
THE BRAIN

Compared to his size, Stegosaurus' brain was very small. It was about the size of a golf ball.

21

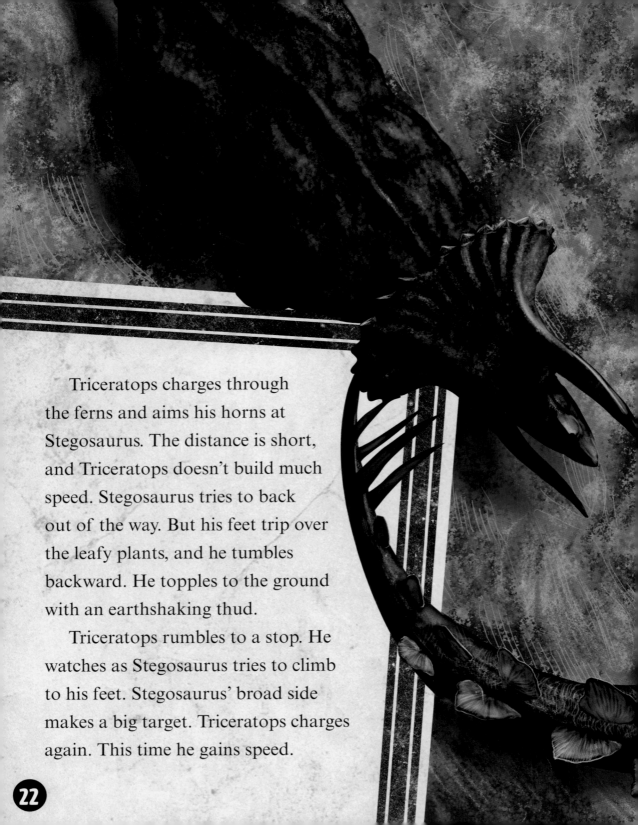

Triceratops charges through
the ferns and aims his horns at
Stegosaurus. The distance is short,
and Triceratops doesn't build much
speed. Stegosaurus tries to back
out of the way. But his feet trip over
the leafy plants, and he tumbles
backward. He topples to the ground
with an earthshaking thud.

Triceratops rumbles to a stop. He
watches as Stegosaurus tries to climb
to his feet. Stegosaurus' broad side
makes a big target. Triceratops charges
again. This time he gains speed.

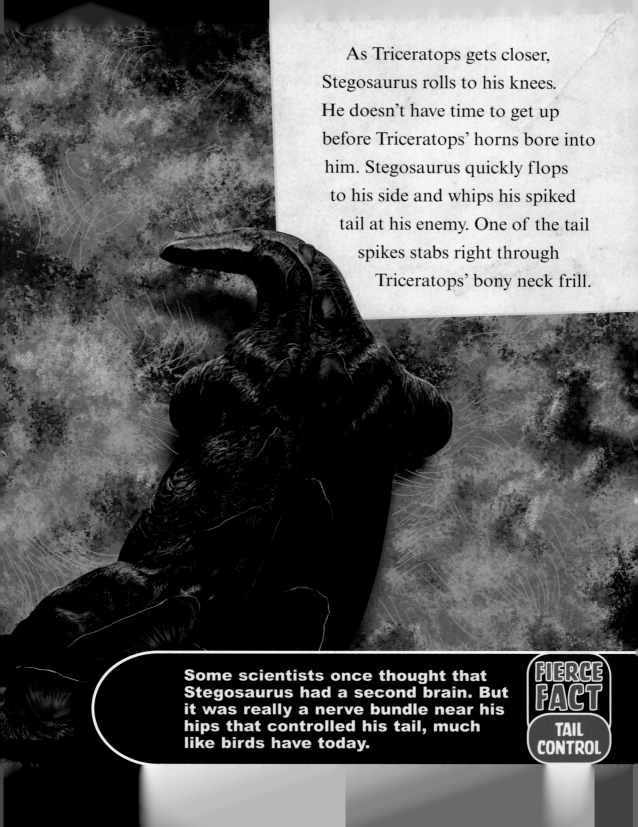

As Triceratops gets closer, Stegosaurus rolls to his knees. He doesn't have time to get up before Triceratops' horns bore into him. Stegosaurus quickly flops to his side and whips his spiked tail at his enemy. One of the tail spikes stabs right through Triceratops' bony neck frill.

Some scientists once thought that Stegosaurus had a second brain. But it was really a nerve bundle near his hips that controlled his tail, much like birds have today.

FIERCE FACT

TAIL CONTROL

As Stegosaurus rolls back to his feet, his spike remains stuck in his opponent's frill. Triceratops wails and jerks his massive head from side to side. As he does, he yanks Stegosaurus' tail. Stegosaurus is pulled off balance and lands on his side again.

FIERCE FACT

FOSSILS

Several fossils of meat-eating dinosaurs have holes that match Stegosaurus' tail spikes.

Triceratops' eyes blaze. He charges once more.
But this time, he runs away from his opponent. As he
bolts, he drags Stegosaurus behind him. Stegosaurus
tries to stop his enemy, but he can't find a firm
footing. He zigzags and bounces behind Triceratops.
A cloud of dirt billows behind the two giant beasts.

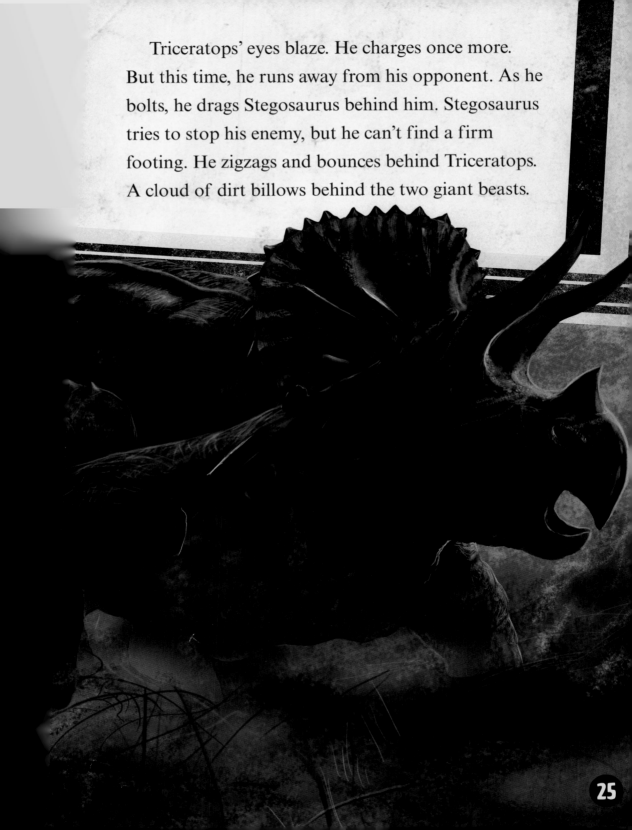

Triceratops dashes wildly out of the clearing, trampling through the bushes. He charges through a small stream, slips, and crashes headfirst to the ground. Stegosaurus tumbles to a stop next to him. Stegosaurus' tail is still lodged in Triceratops' frill. Triceratops opens his sharp beak and bites down hard on his enemy's tail.

Stegosaurus screeches and rips his tail out of Triceratops' beak. Triceratops' head is yanked into the muddy stream bank. Stegosaurus' spike is finally freed.

Stegosaurus climbs to his feet. He lashes wildly with his spikes. He grazes Triceratops' hind leg, ripping open a long, bloody gash. Triceratops bellows. Bloody and angry, Triceratops rises to his feet. He stares furiously at Stegosaurus and backs away. Stegosaurus swipes again with his tail. But the blow doesn't hit — it's just a warning.

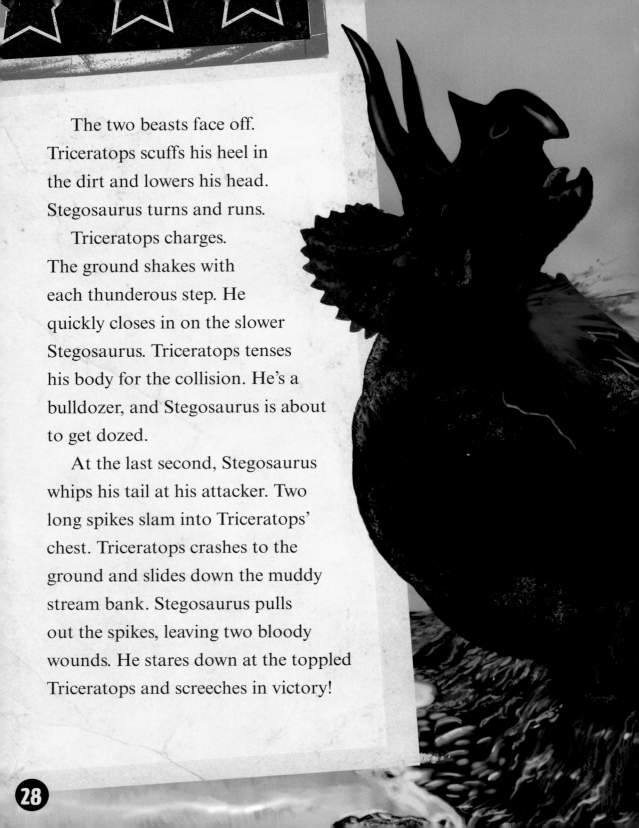

The two beasts face off. Triceratops scuffs his heel in the dirt and lowers his head. Stegosaurus turns and runs.

Triceratops charges. The ground shakes with each thunderous step. He quickly closes in on the slower Stegosaurus. Triceratops tenses his body for the collision. He's a bulldozer, and Stegosaurus is about to get dozed.

At the last second, Stegosaurus whips his tail at his attacker. Two long spikes slam into Triceratops' chest. Triceratops crashes to the ground and slides down the muddy stream bank. Stegosaurus pulls out the spikes, leaving two bloody wounds. He stares down at the toppled Triceratops and screeches in victory!

The name Stegosaurus means "roof lizard."

FIERCE FACT
NAME

GLOSSARY

evolve (ee-VAHLV) — to develop over a long time with gradual changes

extinct (ik-STINGKT) — no longer living; an extinct animal is one whose kind has died out completely.

fossil (FAH-suhl) — the remains or traces of plants and animals that are preserved as rock

frill (FRIL) — a bony collar that fans out around an animal's neck

herbivore (HUR-buh-vor) — an animal that eats only plants

keratin (KAIR-uh-tin) — the hard substance that forms hair and fingernails; some dinosaurs had horns covered with keratin.

pivot (PIV-uht) — to turn on a central point

predator (PRED-uh-tur) — an animal that hunts other animals for food

species (SPEE-sheez) — a group of plants or animals that share common characteristics

READ MORE

Johnson, Jinny. *Dino Wars: Discover the Deadliest Dinosaurs, Bloodiest Battles, and Super Survival Strategies of the Prehistoric World.* New York: Abrams Books for Young Readers, 2005.

Malam, John. *Dinosaur Atlas: An Amazing Journey Through a Lost World.* New York: DK, 2006.

Shone, Rob. *Triceratops: The Three Horned Dinosaur.* Graphic Dinosaurs. New York: PowerKids Press, 2008.

INTERNET SITES

FactHound offers a safe, fun way to find Internet sites related to this book. All of the sites on FactHound have been researched by our staff.

Here's all you do:

Visit *www.facthound.com*

FactHound will fetch the best sites for you!

INDEX